THE PREPARATION OF A QUEEN

Mary A. Covington

Copyright © 2021 Mary A. Covington

Queensation. All Rights Reserved.

All rights are reserved. No parts of this book may be used or reproduced in any manner whatsoever without written permission of the author, except in the case of brief quotations and reviews.

All scripture quotations were taken from the New Living Translation version of the Holy Bible.

First Edition 2020

ISBN 978-0-578-85145-7

The Royal Contents

Introduction: What Exactly Is A Queen.................... 1

Chapter One: Lessons From A Queen 7

Chapter Two: Think Like A Queen........................ 15

Chapter Three: Healing From The Past.................. 23

Chapter Four: The Need For Naomi 31

Chapter Five: Purification of the Queen 40

Introduction

What Exactly Is A Queen?

"Every woman is a queen, and we all have different things to offer."-Queen Latifah

---

As the quote says by Queen Latifah, every woman is a queen. However, not all of them have been reinstated into their queenship. A queen is a part of a royal priesthood. The bible declares that we are a chosen people, a royal priesthood, a holy nation, God's special possession, that we may declare the praises of Him who called us out of darkness into His wonderful light according to 1 Peter 2:9.

By definition a queen is a female ruler especially one who inherits the position by right of birth. Sis, that is you! You have inherited your queenship by being born again in Jesus Christ.

A queen is a woman who knows her purpose, pursues her visions, and plans to take action to accomplish her every goal. She is not afraid of failure because she understands that failure is an opportunity for learning and growth. No one succeeds without first failing.

Her heart is pure and her love for others is impeccable. She does things for others before herself and applauds others who win because she knows that one individual's success is good for the betterment of the team. She is never a slave to her emotions, but the ruler of them. She has great temperament and displays exceptional deportment and poise.

A queen places value on the relationships in her life. She understands that no one can survive as an island, but we were created with a need for relationships with others. The relationships she builds are always strategic and she knows how to prioritize them correctly. She understands that there is good in everyone and that no one is as bad as the worst act that they have done. She limits her judgement and opens her understanding to the root causes of the characteristics of others. Therefore, never having a preconceived opinion of someone, but always giving them the opportunity to prove themselves.

Queens have presence. When she enters a room, she knows that she is not alone, even if she entered it all by herself. She invites the Spirit of God with her wherever she goes and allows Him to lead her. The confidence she has in herself and in her God radiates and encompasses the room. The beauty of her soul captures everyone that she comes in contact with and leaves a lasting impression. Her smile encourages others and disarms the power of any enemy that may come up against her. Love is her driving force. Purpose is her reason. The vision is her goal. Serving others is her heart's desire.

Every queen must understand and know what Psalm 46:5 declares,

"God is in the midst of her, she shall not be moved."

What Exactly Is A Queen?

Which relationships in your life do you need to work on?

_____

_____

_____

_____

_____

Are you aware of your life's purpose?

If so, write it here.

_____

_____

_____

_____

_____

Has God given you a vision for your life?

If so, write the vision and make it plain in the space provided.

_____

_____

_____

_____

_____

CHAPTER ONE

LESSONS FROM A QUEEN

"If I perish let me perish." -Queen Esther

The one queen that I love and learn so much from is Esther. She unveils so much strength, bravery, love, and compassion. Her faith was extremely strong in God and she trusted Him with everything within her. She was so selfless and willing to lay it all on the line for the lives of the Jewish people.

Let's start with the lesson of *FAVOR*. Esther's life wasn't one of privilege or easy times. She was raised by her cousin because her mother and father were deceased. Imagine being a young girl and losing both parents and now having to be raised by a man- that can teach you nothing about being a lady.

When Ester was brought to the palace as a candidate to be the next queen, she immediately obtained favor with the guy that was responsible for the care of the ladies. But first, let's take a moment and think about the fact that she was a candidate! I mean this young girl has experienced loss, hurt, and displacement. Now she is being brought to the palace among other young ladies to be the potential next queen. Who have thought that to be?

Anyway, Esther, because of the favor on her life, was given her things for purification and her seven maidens. Not only that though, she and her maidens were given the best spot in the house where the women and their maidens were being housed. She was given preferential treatment upon entering the palace!

That's why they say,

"favor ain't fair."

Of course, she obtained favor from the king himself as well. King Ahasuerus admired Esther and fell in love upon her coming into his royal palace. Although Esther was very beautiful and nicely shaped it was the favor of God that caused her to be chosen from the rest of the ladies. She hadn't taken anything extra with her into the palace for her one night with the king, except what was recommended. She went in just as she was and was crowned Queen by the King himself.

As we see from the life of Queen Esther, favor doesn't have anything to do with your background, your history, or your past. Favor can't be bought or earned. It is a gift from God that no one can ever take from you.

The next lesson is *CONFIDENCE*. Esther, unlike the other beautiful ladies that were candidates to be queen, believed in her natural self. She was confident in the woman that God created her to be, to win over the king.

The ladies were given whatever it was they wanted to take with them for their one night with the king. Esther asked for nothing. She trusted in God. She knew that if the queenship was for her, she would get it.

That should be your attitude. Know that you are always enough. You don't have to be extra or someone you are not to obtain the blessing of the Lord. Actually, you need to be your authentic self in order to receive the blessing. God favors you- not who you try or pretend to be.

In a room full of beautiful women, you are still able to shine in your own light. In the boardroom with a room full of masterminds you are among the most intellectual. In a room full of millionaires, you are equally wealthy- through Christ!

Lesson number three is *DISCRETION*. Queen Esther was very good at using discretion. She was told by her cousin not to reveal her family background or her race to anyone under any circumstances. Esther was very careful to be obedient and keep these things a secret.

As a queen you must learn to not reveal too much information. It is important to know what information to release at what particular time (if any). There is absolutely no reason to reveal more than what is needed at any given time or in any circumstance. A queen knows that she must keep some things between her and God.

Let's not confuse using discretion as being secretive. Using discretion requires the use of discernment. You have to learn to discern who to release things to and when to release things. Discretion comes from a place of love, positivity, and wisdom.

Secrecy is the act of hiding something. A secret can be kept from someone who may need the information, but it can also be kept from someone who doesn't need the information revealed to them. A secret can be kept as a form of deceit. Queens are not deceptive. She is honest and trustworthy which is the opposite.

The next lesson from Queen Esther is *COURAGE*. There came a time that Queen Esther had to reveal who she was to the king as far as being a Jew. She did this at a banquet that she set up for the king and Haman (the evil man who wanted to take all of the Jews out). At the banquet Esther made a request that her life and the life of her people be spared.

She knew the danger of it all. However, her courageous act saved a whole race of people. As queens we must understand that we are on the front lines. As leaders we must sometimes take risks that may put us in unfavorable positions to save others or make situations better for others. Because of Esther's courage the Jews were exalted, able to celebrate, and were given the power and authority to slay their enemies!

Let these lessons from Queen Esther sink in. In order for you to be impactful you must be favored by the Lord, confident, use discretion, and be very courageous. Remember, you have been chosen for this. Walk in the authority and power that God has given you, through His son Jesus Christ. I see you, girl!

Lessons From A Queen

Queens are confident. What will you commit to doing as of today to boost your self-confidence?

_____

_____

_____

_____

_____

_____

_____

_____

_____

_____

_____

Chapter Two

Think Like a Queen

Anything is possible with the correct mindset, passion, and diligence.

-Mary A. Covington

Queen, we must often be renewed in our minds! Romans 12:2 reminds us to not be conformed to the patterns (ways) of the world. If we are renewed in our minds, we will be able to know what is God's will for our lives. For it is His will that is good and perfect-always!

Thinking like a queen is not an ability we are born with. We must constantly practice this behavior to perfect it. As the old saying goes,

"Practice makes perfect!"

Focus is very important in maintaining the mindset of a queen. Whatever feeds your focus will ultimately consume your time. Therefore, we must focus on the things that take preeminence in our lives. These things should be those that improve, elevate, and add value.

Prioritizing things in your life will be extremely helpful here. What is most important to you? Is it your education, parenting, career, marriage, or something else? In any case you should create a plan to help achieve these things and be committed to working persistently on getting it done so you can move on to the next thing.

THE PREPARATION OF A QUEEN

Queens must be forward thinkers. She has to always have a plan for the future. She is never stagnant, but always moving forward in an innovative way. Her vision is big enough for others to grab a hold of and run with it. She strives to learn new things, often so she can empower others and improve the condition of life for those connected to her.

Control is not in the nature of a queen. She values the opinions, ideas, and input of others. She loves teamwork and what's best for the majority, rather than herself alone.

Forward thinking requires meditation. You must get by yourself sometimes and sit and think. Playing some relaxing instrumental music can help with this as well. When a queen takes the time to think she is always prepared to make courageous, bold- calculated risks.

The growth mindset of a queen allows her to help develop that same mindset in others. The key to this is praising others for their effort rather than for their skill or ability. It's the work that matters because many "can do" they just choose not to.

She knows within herself that her weaknesses can become strengthened overtime with the right development. Queens don't get stuck after a failure because she uses that opportunity as a learning experience, which will encourage growth. Queens understand that life is a mix of wins and losses. However, she believes that growth comes from experience and we are forever students that have to learn daily. With patience and dedication, improvement will be the outcome. It is only when we know better that we can do better. Life is all about principles- a queen knows that!

Because our mindset affects our behavior, a queen knows that she has to stay sharp. There are some things that she must not allow to linger. Unforgiveness is at the top of this list.

THE PREPARATION OF A QUEEN

Queens understand the importance of forgiving others. We can't be expected to be forgiven by the Father if we don't forgive. Unforgiveness is like poison so we can't allow ourselves to die by this evil venom.

When you allow unforgiveness to linger it affects your behavior. Instead of treating the person with love you now treat them unkind and with spitefulness. The treatment may be subtle, but it is still there.

Bitterness sprouts from unforgiveness. Queens cannot be bitter! It is not a good look. In the place of bitterness, you cannot be impactful. Queenship is all about serving others and being a positive influence to those around you.

In your preparation as a queen, you must learn to be stable in your mindset. A double minded queen is unstable in all of her ways. When it comes to decision making, don't move hastily. Always take the time to think things through. Once you have thought about it thoroughly, you then must analyze all possible outcomes. Your decision should reflect the best pragmatic outcome for everyone involved, not just yourself.

The most important thought in this process is written in Philippians 2:5

"Let this mind be in you, which was also in Christ Jesus."

When we put on the mind of Christ, everything else eventually falls into place. Jesus was very purpose driven. He knew what He had to do and He didn't let anything get in the way of its completion.

Jesus asked His parents at the age of twelve years old,

"Why are you searching for me? Didn't you know I had to be about my Father's business?"

At this moment Jesus was in the temple sitting among the religious teachers learning and asking questions. He was getting prepared for His own assignments, although it was nothing the teachers could teach Him because He is the ultimate teacher. He demonstrated to us that we must always remain a student in life. Queens, take pleasure in sitting at the feet of trailblazers to soak up more wisdom and knowledge.

Know your divine assignment and get to work!

Think Like A Queen

Who do you need to forgive?

_____

_____

_____

Write a prayer to God here to begin the process of forgiving those you just listed above.

_____

_____

_____

What assignments do you feel God is calling you to fulfill on the Earth?

_____

_____

_____

Chapter Three

Healing From The Past

One day it will all be ok. Your one day is coming. - K.S.

The past can be the biggest tripwire for someone who isn't focused. Pain has a way of trying to hold onto us and remind us of just how bad things are. It gets in the soul and shatters the hope of all who allows it to do so. The good news is, it eventually has to let go. It stops hurting, but it's up to the individual to allow God to heal the wound.

Queens are made for kings. Eventually he is going to begin his search for you. You wouldn't dare want him to find you in the place of despair, over something that has happened in your past. Also, you don't want him to find you with a Band-Aid over a wound that will start to bleed immediately if touched.

The healing process forces you to be brutally honest with yourself. It may feel like you are attacking yourself, but in reality, you're just getting to the root of the issue. Roots are deep. To get to them it takes a lot of probing and digging.

It takes asking yourself the hard questions to begin to heal. Along with the hard questions must come the hard truth. For instance, if your pain is from a previous romantic relationship you may have to ask yourself,

"Why did I get with him in the first place?"

Now, I know your immediate response may be

"Because I liked him."

Even so, you must understand that this question is taking you back to day one. What state of mind were you in the day you guys said hello?

When you started dating him did you like him? Was he just a convenient option? Were you desperate for love? On the rebound? Backsliding? Being spiteful?

These are just examples and possibilities. I want you to really think about it and be one hundred percent honest with yourself. The things you don't acknowledge can't be healed.

Let's go here as well. Ask yourself,

"Why did I stay after he hurt me more than once?"

A queen's heart must be pure and whole. How can she give her king her heart if it's in one million pieces? King David, in the Bible, asked God to create in him a clean heart and renew a right spirit within him. Things happen that causes our heart to be dispositioned. Our spirits become tainted from the things we go through in life. That's why, queens, we must pray constantly for the purification of our hearts and spirits. We can only be the best versions of ourselves if we are pure in heart.

In Proverbs, King Solomon put it like this,

"A happy heart is good medicine and a joyful mind causes healing, but a broken spirit dries up the bones."

As a queen you can't afford to walk around all broken and disheartened. You must begin to take the necessary steps to become whole, healed, and happy.

Here are a few ways that you can start.

1. Share your emotions with a trusted individual.

Talking out your problems with someone you trust can actually bring you some consolation. You will find that as you open up, you will begin to feel your peace return. A listening ear is healthy because we all want to feel like someone cares and we're not all alone. Venting can be therapeutic.

2. Don't obsess over the situation.

Reliving the situation constantly over and over in your mind will only cause you agony. You have to learn to let it rest. Understand that no matter how much you think about it, it's not going to undo the hurt. It will only make it worse.

3. Pray & journal your thoughts daily.

Journaling will be a huge part of your healing process. There are times you will have to pray and write. You don't want to overwhelm others with your situation. So, journaling will help balance out the amount of human console you will need. When you write let all of the hurt out on the pages. Be totally transparent because only you and God will see what you have written.

4. Keep yourself interested in life.

Start going out doing new things. Find a new hobby and also rekindle the passion for the ones you already have. Create something new. Watch comedy movies or your favorite tv series. Try new and exciting activities with friends and family. Take a mini vacation to a city you never visited or stay at a hotel resort with a lot of amenities.

Healing may also mean discontinuing all forms of communication with a person. That doesn't mean you have ill feelings towards them, but it creates the space you need to clear your mind and your heart of the hurt. Oftentimes, individuals can be reminded of the pain someone caused every time they see the offender. It's like reliving the hurt. Sometimes distance is part of the prescription for healing.

Checking your offender's social media accounts doesn't help anything, it only adds more time onto your healing process. The quicker you process the saying *out of sight, out of mind* the better off things will be for you.

5. Level up your self-care & self-love

There is nothing like doing things for yourself that make you happy. These things may include beauty enhancements such as: hair appointments, professional makeup, spa treatments, and body waxing.

Getting a biweekly manicure and pedicure may help you feel better as well. If it's not in your budget to get these things done professionally, you can always do them yourself. Taking the time to do your nails will ease your mind and result in you feeling better about yourself.

We know as women we feel great when we look great- no matter what else is going on in our lives! Don't cheat yourself by neglecting your self-care.

As for self-love this is vital. Queen, love yourself like you expect your king to love you. Do things for yourself that you want your king to take up when he comes along. Remember, we aren't looking to be saved by a man we are expecting him to add to what we have already established.

Self-love looks like dating yourself. Take yourself to your favorite restaurant-alone. Go shopping and splurge on yourself every once in a while, (when you have saved up the money). Treat yourself like the queen you are and that way your king will already know what type of act he has to follow in order to win you over. Set the bar high, Queen!

As part of your preparation, you have to get to know yourself very well. Learn to enjoy your own company. Also, during your time of preparation it is important that you develop a strong relationship with God. You must become intimate with Him and delight yourself in Him. When you delight yourself in Him, He in return will give you the desires of your heart.

Chapter Four

The Need For Naomi

"We make a living by what we get, we make a life by what we give." - Winston Churchill

---

In the Holy Bible there is a story about a young lady named Ruth and her mother-in-law Naomi. This is a very famous account in the Bible especially among women because of Boaz, the man that Ruth ultimately marries. However, I want us to take a closer look at Naomi and the relationship between her and Ruth.

First, let's get the backstory out of the way. Naomi was a widow who had suffered the loss of her husband first and then her two sons and all that she had. Ruth was married to one of her sons and she had another daughter-in-law by the name of Orpah.

Now that she was alone with just her daughters-in-law, Naomi decided to go back to her homeland, Judah. Initially, she was taking the young ladies with her. Nevertheless, somewhere along the journey Naomi suggested to the girls to go back home to their mothers. She spoke blessings over their lives, showered them with love, and showed gratitude for the things they had done for her. She wept with them because the separation would be bittersweet. Orpah went on her way, back home to her mother, but Ruth stayed with Naomi.

Ruth clung to Naomi. She said to her,

"Don't ask me to leave you and turn back. Wherever you go, I will go; wherever you live I will live. Your people will be my people and your God will be my God. Wherever you die, I will die, and there I will be buried. May the Lord

punish me severely if I allow anything but death to separate us!"

Why does every Queen need a Naomi? We all need a spiritual mother that can cover us and give us wise and godly counsel. This woman should have experience in life and has gained wisdom that she is willing to share, to help us avoid pitfalls and wandering in the wilderness of life.

Every queen needs to be able to glean from a queen who has her best interest at heart. Someone who has spiritual insight and revelation that will put her in a better position. Naomi knew when it was time to arise and move from the place of little to the place of provision. She took responsibility for the young ladies Ruth and Orpah and decided to shift and move forward for them all. She was a strong leader with a heart for the ladies.

She didn't envy the young women. She understood that she was too old to enter into another marriage, but she encouraged them to move on with their lives.

Naomi, was a woman of faith, strength, and compassion. She understood when it was time to release the girls, and not hold them back or tie them down because they were once married to her sons. She knew when and how to release them. She spoke blessings and not curses. She spoke life and not death. She spoke peace and prosperity.

Naomi had influence on Ruth. She had lived a life that demonstrated faith, strength, and love to Ruth. She was able to get Ruth to convert to believing in the one and only true living God. Remember, Ruth said to her,

"Your God will be my God."

With love and kindness, she won Ruth over! Naomi also saw something in Ruth as well. It was only after Ruther began to cling to Naomi and show her that she was determined to stay with her that Naomi moved forward towards Judah.

In chapter 3 of the book of Ruth, Naomi gives Ruth instructions and wise counsel on what to do concerning Boaz. Ruth, with boldness and confidence, followed the instructions she was given. She didn't deviate from them at all. By doing exactly what Ruth told her, she in the end was blessed & highly favored.

Because of Ruth's faithfulness to Naomi and all the respect, love, and care that she had given her, she reaped blessings and favor. Boaz, a man of wealth and influence chose Ruth as his wife. She was able to get the king she deserved by being faithful.

Queens, don't take your Naomi for granted. Bless her whenever possible. Pray for her, listen to her, and never deviate from the instructions that she gives you. In due season you will reap a reward for your obedience.

One last important thing to note is that Ruth chose Naomi and not vice versa.

Here are a few tips on choosing the Naomi for you:

1. She must be a woman of God.

2. She must have spiritual insight and revelatory wisdom.

3. Her lifestyle must match her words and line up with the Word of God

4. Her heart needs to be pure and full of love and compassion.

5. She must be stronger than you spiritually and currently operating on a level you desire to get to.

6. Check her spiritual fruit.

7. Be sure to take it to God in prayer and wait for an answer before moving forward with your decision.

8. She must be a woman of prayer.

9. She must be full of the Word and able to give wise counsel based on biblical principles.

10. Integrity is key! You must be able to trust her undoubtedly.

Your Naomi will be your destiny helper! She will push, encourage, and rebuke you with love. She will only want the best for you and her desire will be to see you thrive and excel in life. There will never be any contentment, jealousy, envy, or covetousness that comes from her; only love, compassion, and strength.

The Need For Naomi

Write a sincere prayer to God asking Him to send His ordained Naomi for your life to you.

_____
_____
_____
_____
_____
_____
_____
_____
_____
_____
_____
_____

THE PREPARATION OF A QUEEN

Chapter Five

Purification of the Queen

The real ornament of a woman is her character; her purity. -Mahatma Gandhi

---

Queens, like Esther, must go through a process of purification. The first step in this process is being washed in the blood of Jesus Christ. Yes, you must accept Christ as your personal saviour first and foremost.

Giving Jesus your *"Yes"* is the first day of the rest of your life.

After this, you will go through the continued process of deliverance. This process never ends because there is always something that we must be delivered from. However, the part I'm referring to here is putting off the old man (your past). During your process you will be made more and more into the image of Jesus Christ.

Once you accept Christ old things are passed away and behold all things become new!

Purification is the process of distilling all errors that have been attached to you in any form in your mind, body, and soul.

To purify the mind is to cleanse the spirit of all fowl and negative thoughts and opinions. The most important way to do this is by reading the Bible faithfully. It is also good to ask the Father to renew a right spirit within you during prayer- daily. Be sure to limit what goes into your mind. Be careful of the music you listen to, what you watch with your eyes, and what you read as well. Erotica books are not good for queens who are trying to live a holy and righteous life.

In Romans 12:1, the Apostle Paul writes,

"And so, dear brothers and sisters, I plead with you to give your bodies to God because of all He has done for you. Let them be a living and holy sacrifice- the kind that He will find acceptable."

To present your body a living sacrifice to God means to dedicate and entrust it to God. You are giving your body over to Him to be used by Him for His own purpose. You must do this every day in the presence of the Lord.

The moment you decided to do this your flesh will begin to go to war with your spirit. The flesh wants what it wants so it doesn't want you to sacrifice it totally to God. Therefore, queen, you are going to have to constantly battle until the victory is won!

Another part of this process is purifying the heart. The heart is so important. The Bible says,

"Blessed are the pure in heart, for they shall see God."

If your heart isn't pure queen, you will ultimately miss Heaven. What in this world is worth that? Nothing at all!

Ask the Lord to create in you a clean heart every single day. There are so many scriptures about the heart. You may be asking how do you keep your heart pure. I would suggest prayer, much forgiveness, and the D.A.D. method.

We talked briefly about one of the D's in the D.A.D method in a previous chapter. The first *"D"* stands for dwell.

Dwell means to live in or at a specific place. We must live in the presence of God. In the presence of God there is the fullness of joy. In His presence there is peace and serenity. It's in His presence that we get instruction and strategy. Live to dwell in Him.

The *"A"* stands for abide. This means to remain. We must allow Christ to abide in us as we remain in Him. In Him is everything that we could ever need, want, or desire.

The last *"D"* stands for delight. We must take pleasure in doing the will of the Lord. We must witness and disciple others daily. Delighting in Him means we are selfless. This is when we put our stuff to the side and take full pleasure in the Lord and what He needs from us.

If you implement the D.A.D method you will reach a new level and get to know God like never before. You won't be swayed by the blustering winds that sometimes blow in life. You will be able to stand against the evil of the devil and all of his tactics and lies.

How are you planning to put the D.A.D method into play? There is no greater pleasure than to know that you are pleasing the Father. How can you be ready for your king and you haven't taken pleasure in the King of all Kings?

In your preparation I pray that you become the Queen that God has predestined you to be. Take your rightful place. There are so many people that are counting on you. People you have and have not met. Others, you may never get the chance to meet, either way your life will be a testimony unto them.

Stay focused queen and know that you have been handpicked. You are favored and you are loved!

Stay Connected

For more Queen resources:

Join the *Royal Blitz Challenge-*

This is a 5-day mini course on getting things in order before your king arrives. It is a great way to add more value to your queenship. You can find the signup form on Bit.ly/royalblitz

Facebook Group: Queens Pray

Facebook Page: Queensation

Instagram: queensation_mary

Join the book club: Queens Read Book Club

Sign up on the Queensation Facebook page or in the Facebook group

Join the email list: bit.ly/queensation

Email: marycovington@queensation.com

Programs & Products

The Preparation of a Queen Program

This program is an extension of the contents of this book. We dive deeper into key topics that will expand your knowledge on living like royalty-just as God intended.

To sign up visit: bit.ly/queenprep

Other Programs include:

The Visualization Mentorship Program

A 30-day intensive training program that transforms and elevates the mindset, while assisting with execution of purpose driven visions in queens like yourself.

www.ingramcontent.com/pod-product-compliance
Lightning Source LLC
Chambersburg PA
CBHW072038060426
42449CB00010BA/2338